WISDOM
FROM THE
PROVERBS

Dan and Nancy Dick

Edited by Trudie Martineau

BARBOUR
PUBLISHING

WISDOM
FROM THE
PROVERBS

ISBN 1-58660-739-1

Scripture quotations are taken from the King James Version of the Bible.

Published by Barbour Publishing, Inc., P.O. Box 719, Uhrichsville, Ohio 44683, www.barbourbooks.com

Our mission is to publish and distribute inspirational products offering exceptional value and biblical encouragement to the masses.

Printed in the United States of America.
5 4 3 2 1

DAY I

The proverbs of Solomon the son of David,
king of Israel. . .to give subtilty to the simple,
to the young man knowledge and discretion (1:1, 4).

The saying is certainly true which says "Experience is the best teacher." It is through day-to-day living that we come to understand life. What we did not understand as children we come to know as adults. When we start upon a new endeavor we learn slowly, gathering more information and experience until we finally master it.

Our Christian life is like that. We start out inexperienced and with little knowledge, but then we grow in our understanding and commitment. Christ Himself spent a good deal of His life preparing for His ministry and work. Like Him, we are growing, maturing, and preparing for the kingdom of God, which awaits us. When we search for God in the Bible and through prayer we are being made ready for our heavenly home. In this life, we never really arrive at "being" Christian, but we are ever "becoming" Christian. As long as we continue to learn, we continue to grow. In that growth lies wisdom.

PRAYER: Dear heavenly Father, grant that I might continue to learn more about You each and every day. Create in me a real hunger for Your truth. Amen.

DAY 2

The fear of the LORD is the beginning of knowledge: but fools despise wisdom and instruction (1:7).

Standing on the shore of a great ocean, one is amazed at the force of the waves crashing on the rocks. The vast expanse of water is awe inspiring, yet it is beautiful. Only a very foolish person would ignore the dangers presented by the sea, yet, only a fool would not be attracted by its beauty. The ocean is to be feared and respected, but it is also to be experienced. Despite our sense of awe, or perhaps because of it, we are drawn to the water, to be immersed in it, to become part of it. Our true enjoyment of the surf comes when we enter in, but only when we understand its power.

The same is true of God. We stand in awe before Him, wisely cautious in the face of His power, yet we long to know Him, to be united with Him. The wise pursue Him with all their heart, while the foolish ignore Him or reject Him through their fear. Once we understand the power of our Lord, this fear enables us to be with Him, immersed in Him, but always respecting His might.

PRAYER: O Lord, help me to know fear in a positive way, and set my feet on the path to wisdom. Amen.

DAY 3

So are the ways of every one that is greedy of gain; which taketh away the life of the owners thereof (1:19).

An important question each person should ask is "How much do I really need?" Christ is quite clear about the accumulation of wealth. As in the story of the man who built his storehouses bigger to hold his great crops, Christ asks each one of us where it is we keep our treasure. Is it on earth, or is it in heaven? Surely God wants every person to enjoy life and to share in good times, but He does not find joy in the celebration of a few when many suffer.

A good guideline to follow concerning the possessions of this world is to contemplate the question of what Christ might do with the same possessions if they were His. If this rule were followed much more would be given and shared, and fewer people would have to do without. The Bible says that greed is keeping what we don't need. God rejoices in the life of a giver but has no part of the greedy person's life. With His help and guidance, we all can learn to be more giving.

PRAYER: Oh heavenly Father, open my eyes to the needs of those around me. Destroy the spirit of selfishness in my heart, and teach me to give as You would give. Amen.

DAY 4

When your fear cometh as desolation, and your destruction cometh as a whirlwind; when distress and anguish cometh upon you. Then shall they call upon me, but I will not answer; they shall seek me early, but they shall not find me (1:27–28).

A little boy waited patiently, day after day, to be allowed to play baseball with the bigger boys on the block. Every game was the same. He sat waiting and never got to play. One day he didn't bother to show up. He found another team on another block where he was needed. His old team came to find themselves short of the number needed to play, so they called on the little boy. The boy said, "If you wanted me so bad, you should have given me a chance to play before. Now it's too late."

Often we treat God the same way. When things are going well we ignore Him, but the minute things go wrong we run to Him, hoping He will make everything all right. God is not someone we should turn to only in times of trial. He should be a part of our whole life, both in good times and bad. We must be sure to include God in everything we do.

PRAYER: Dear God, forgive those times when I seem to forget You. Help me to include You in all I do, think, and feel. Be with me to guide me, now and forever. Amen.

DAY 5

Then shalt thou understand righteousness, and judgment, and equity; yea, every good path (2:9).

Jesus Christ selected for Himself a band of twelve rough, rugged men to be His disciples. These men knew very little of qualities like gentleness, compassion, kindness, and giving. Prior to Jesus coming to them they had very little reason to consider any of these traits. Their paths were many, but none would have been considered good. None until Christ came along.

During their three years with Jesus, the disciples learned everything there was to know of these qualities. They came to understand all that Jesus tried to show them. They carried these qualities of goodness into the world and taught others to follow them.

If we will take time to spend with Christ, through prayer, Bible reading, and devotion, we too will learn these traits. We will learn to follow the good paths that Jesus followed. This is what it means to be a Christian. The key is in spending time with God in order to learn them.

PRAYER: Remind me, heavenly Father, that I should spend time with You today and every day. Make me a disciple of Yours, anxious to learn all You would teach me. Amen.

DAY 6

To deliver thee from the way of the evil man,
from the man that speaketh froward things;
who leave the paths of uprightness,
to walk in the ways of darkness; who rejoice to do evil,
and delight in the frowardness of the wicked (2:12–14).

I recently visited a woman in the hospital. She didn't seem too happy to see me, and after awhile she let me know why. "God is doing this to me," she said. "He is punishing me because I'm not a church woman. He just waits for someone to make a mistake, then He gets them."

Isn't it strange that people think of God this way? God doesn't want anyone to suffer. He never punishes people arbitrarily. Nor does He turn His sight from those who do wrong. God will finally be the judge of all people, and true justice will be served, but to think that God acts unfairly and without cause is absurd. God loves all human beings and wants the best for them. His love knows no bounds, and when we suffer or struggle, He struggles with us. God is with us in both good times and bad, but He is never to be blamed for our misfortunes. Instead, He is to be praised and thanked for all the wonderful blessings we receive each and every day. There is no place we can go that God will not be with us. This is the real meaning of blessed assurance. God is with us. Hallelujah!

PRAYER: O thank You, dear Lord, that I am never out of Your sight. You are with me always. Grant that I might feel Your presence each and every day. It is good to know I am never alone. Amen.

DAY 7

*But the wicked shall be cut off from the earth,
and the transgressors shall be rooted out of it (2:22).*

So often it seems like the evil will inherit the earth, rather than the meek. Bad people with evil intentions appear blessed in many ways that good people are not. It is a hard lesson to learn that the rain falls on the just and the unjust alike. Often it would be so nice to see the unkind, cruel, hateful people get what they deserve. Like God's people throughout history, we cry out for God to bring justice upon the heads of our persecutors.

In due time God will do just that. God's time is not our time, however, and we must learn to be patient and wait. God offers us a helpful suggestion in waiting for justice to come. Jesus says, "Judge not lest ye be judged. Why beholdest thou the mote that is in thy brother's eye, but considerest not the beam that is in thine own eye?" It is easy to sit back and hope for other people to receive their just desserts, but what God wants us to do is make sure we are doing everything we should be doing. Justice is God's responsibility. Ours is to do those things which we know are pleasing to God and to avoid doing the things which He dislikes—like judging our neighbors.

PRAYER: Help me be patient and turn from bitter feelings toward those who do wrong. Let me love them with Your love, and help me look at my own life to see that it is pleasing in Your sight. Amen.

DAY 8

Honour the LORD with thy substance,
and with the firstfruits of all thine increase:
So shall thy barns be filled with plenty,
and thy presses shall burst out with new wine. (3:9–10).

Two men stood at the gate of a great city. While they waited, a poor woman came to them asking for a few coins with which she could buy bread for her children. The first man scowled at the woman and said, "I work hard for my money. I give of my own time and my own labor. I earn what I reap. Go and do the same for yourself and your family!" The woman began to walk away, but the other man followed after her and said, "Poor woman, take this money, for it is not really mine. I do work hard for it, but it is by God's grace that I have it at all. He gave me the talents I possess; He gave me my strength and knowledge; and He has given to us all the lives we have to live. If I give to you, I simply give to God what He has provided."

It is good to remember that without God we would not possess the things we do. All things come to us from God, and it is good that we share them. Jesus told the people that whenever they came to the aid of another person in need, they were in fact aiding Him. True prosperity comes only when we learn to give to others as freely as God gives to us.

PRAYER: Oh Father, soften my heart to those who are less fortunate than I am. Help me to appreciate the blessings I have been given and to share from my abundance. Fill me with the new wine, which is Your Spirit. Amen.

DAY 9

Length of days is in her right hand;
and in her left hand riches and honour (3:16).

Wisdom—the knowledge of God—is a gift from God. He gives it to all people who come to Him seeking true understanding. He will not deny it to anyone, but He will give it in small enough portions to enable the individual to make sense of it. As a person comes to know God better, he or she will avoid those activities which are self-destructive and unprofitable. The person receives a deeper appreciation of the wonder of God in the world. Life becomes more meaningful, and the person gains a new understanding of what it means to be a success.

Life is a privilege which God wants us to value. When we turn from Him and pursue our own selfish desires, we lose sight of the sacredness of His gift. We may think that we can find fulfillment in life on our own, but it is through God and God alone that we can come to know the wonder of life most fully. God is the author of life, and He will bless us with its richness if we will only let Him. A full and happy life, rich in meaning and honorable in all ways, is the prize of any believer who will keep God centered in his or her life.

PRAYER: Help me to see the beauty and wonder of this life You have given to me, O Lord. Open my eyes so that I might come to know the richness and fullness You intend my life to have. Grant me this, I pray. Amen.

DAY 10

*Be not afraid of sudden fear,
neither of the desolation of the wicked,
when it cometh. For the LORD shall be thy confidence,
and shall keep thy foot from being taken (3:25–26).*

A teacher returned to her classroom to find chaos had broken out. Paper, pencils, and erasers were flying through the air, pictures were drawn on the blackboards and walls, children were running all around the room, and the noise was deafening. One little girl sat quietly in the back corner, refusing to enter into the mischief. As the teacher began to scold the class, she remembered the little girl who was well behaved. After class, she pulled the young child aside and told her how much it meant to her that she had remained silent and obedient.

Often we feel as though our good acts are missed. When we don't receive credit and acclaim, we feel cheated. What we need to remember is that none of our actions go unnoticed by God. He sees our every move, and He applauds us when we refuse to do those things we know we should not, but that our society seems to approve of. Our reward will never come from this life, but from the life that awaits us with our heavenly Father. His blessing is ever with us if we will only be patient and believe.

PRAYER: Father, often I feel as though my good behavior is ignored or forgotten. Forgive me for being prideful, and help me to know that You see me at both my best and worst and love me all the time. Amen.

DAY 11

Withhold not good from them to whom it is due,
when it is in the power of thine hand to do it. Say not
unto thy neighbour, Go, and come again, and to morrow
I will give; when thou hast it by thee (3:27–28).

Recently I had a flat tire while I was on a busy interstate. I tried to flag down passing cars, hoping for some assistance. Hundreds of cars passed without even slowing down. I began to think of all the times I had passed motorists in distress, and I didn't have the time or the inclination to help them. I felt a little guilty, and it made me much more understanding of those who whizzed past. It also made me much more appreciative of the help when it came.

We are given so many opportunities in our lives to help other people in need. It is important that we reach out and take hold of those chances. Jesus said that every time we help any person in need, it is as if we have done it for Christ Himself. It is easy to decide whether or not we would help Christ. Should it be any more difficult to decide whether or not we should help another of God's children, especially when Christ equated them to Himself? If we have the means to help those in need, there really is no choice. We are called to serve others as Christ was willing to serve us. We must do this when we see the opportunity.

PRAYER: Lord, so often I turn my head from those in need. Open my eyes and my heart that I might reach out to them, to extend the hand of Christ to those who themselves are Christ. Amen.

DAY 12

For the froward is abomination to the LORD:
but his secret is with the righteous (3:32).

There is something exciting and pleasing about being
in on a secret. When we are told secrets, it shows that
we are trusted and esteemed. It makes us special. It
sets us apart. God has made us privy to a very special
secret. We have been given information which can
change our lives. That secret is simple, yet powerful.
God is love, and with Him all things are possible.

This doesn't seem like much of a secret, but it is
amazing how many people act as though they are not
in on it. For those people who devote themselves to
loving and following God, this secret is the greatest joy
of their lives. For those who don't know it, it comes
as the greatest disappointment and torment when it
is revealed. God offers this secret to all people, and it is
the obligation of everyone who knows it to share it with
as many other people as they can. The secret that God
gives to the righteous is a secret that He wants the
whole world to share. The greatest desire of God is a
day when the secret the righteous share will no longer
be a secret. It will be a truth that is known by all.

PRAYER: Lord, grant that I might always and every-
where share the blessed secret of Your love with everyone I
meet. Make me a true disciple of Yours, spreading Your love
and gospel throughout my world. Amen.

DAY 13

Forsake her not, and she shall preserve thee: love her,
and she shall keep thee (4:6).

An older friend of mine always lived by the rule "Let your conscience be your guide." Whenever he was faced by a tough decision, he said, "I stop thinking and I start feeling." For this wise old gentleman, wisdom came from listening not so much to his mind, but more to his heart. He always told me that he knew deep inside whether or not he was making a good choice. Whenever he tried to do what he knew wasn't right, a feeling crept over him, and he could not rest easily until he did what was right.

Truly, God has given us a conscience, a "still small voice," an inner wisdom which guides us and comforts us when we remain true to its instruction. When we choose to ignore the wisdom of our conscience, we face feelings of guilt and anxiety. When we pay close attention to the wisdom of our heart, we find there is special comfort. Doing what we know to be right offers not only freedom from guilt, but also a joy, which comes forth from our soul. Christ rejoices each time we open ourselves to the guidance of the Holy Spirit in our lives. Often God speaks to us through our consciences. If we will listen, God will preserve and keep us.

PRAYER: O heavenly Father, I reach out to Your guidance and will. Fill me with a special wisdom so I might always choose to follow the right path. Shine Your light before me so that I will never stray. Amen.

DAY 14

But the path of the just is as the shining light, that shineth more and more unto the perfect day (4:18).

A young woman worked at a factory which was about ten blocks from where she lived. She could walk to work, but to do so she had to cross a railroad bridge which was treacherous going when the sun began to set. During the winter months it was doubly dangerous due to slippery conditions as well as darkness. The woman would have avoided the crossing altogether had it not been for the crossing guard. Each evening as the woman approached the crossing, the guard waved a lantern to signal that he awaited. Using the powerful light, he would lead the woman by the hand across the bridge. Throughout her life the woman never forgot the kindness and help of the older crossing guard.

The lives of those people who are touched by the love of Christ are like guiding lights to others who have yet to find Christ in their lives. They can provide guidance and help, and they shine forth as bright examples of how good life can be. God's light can shine through us if we will only let it. We have the opportunity to show others the difference that Christ can make. When we live life empowered by the light of God, we live as He wishes we would.

PRAYER: Father, please make me a light for my world. Let me shine forth with Your goodness, care, and love. Let all who look to me see Your grace. Help me to magnify the saving light of Christ which You have lovingly given me. Amen.

DAY 15

Keep thy heart with all diligence;
for out of it are the issues of life (4:23).

Jesus said, "Where your treasure is, there will your heart be also." (Matt. 6:21) What we feel and believe are the truly precious and meaningful things in our lives. If we don't commit ourselves to what is good and right, then we are empty. Moral poverty occurs when we place things above relationships. Christ sent His disciples out into the world without possessions, but no one in history has known more wealth than those chosen men who walked with Jesus. It is when we choose to walk with Jesus that we can find out what true riches are.

In today's world, it is easy to get distracted by so many things. Lifestyles are presented in magazines and on television that seem so appealing. The "good life" requires money, good looks, nice clothes, and the right car, the right house, the right mate. At least, that's what we're supposed to believe. But it is only when we can free ourselves from the pursuit of such things that we can begin to enjoy life the way God intended it. Money cannot buy happiness, nor can it bring us life. Christ brings us life, and He brings it most abundantly. He is the real treasure, and as long as our hearts remain with Him, our lives will truly be rich.

PRAYER: Dear Father, forgive me when I lose sight of what is really important in life. Help me to keep my eyes focused on Your truth. Enable me to show others that You are the real treasure in life. Amen.

DAY 16

Turn not to the right hand nor to the left:
remove thy foot from evil (4:27).

When recently traveling to my sister's house, I found myself hopelessly lost. She had given me good directions, telling me to stay on a highway until I came to a certain traffic light. I drove down the highway for what seemed like hours. As the miles passed, I began to doubt whether or not my sister had given me the right directions. The doubts grew and grew, until finally I decided to turn off. I headed in the general direction I thought my sister would be, and that was how I got myself lost. As it turned out, I was only a few minutes from the proper light, but because of my doubts, I was led to make a bad decision.

Many times in our lives we will find ourselves in situations where we grow impatient or doubtful. It is during those times that it is most important to hold fast to the promises of God. God is always there, and He knows what is best for us in every situation. It is vital that we not turn to the right or left, but stay steadfastly on the path that leads to God. If we will learn to do that, then the blessings of God will be ours in all circumstances.

PRAYER: Almighty God, forgive me when I doubt Your will and guidance. Help me to always have the faith I need to trust and obey. Make me constant in my belief in You. Amen.

DAY 17

*Hear me now therefore, O ye children,
and depart not from the words of my mouth (5:7).*

The sign nailed to the tree said "No Trespassing." The red letters stood out for yards in every direction. But that didn't stop the young boys from climbing the fence in order to reach the apples that grew on the trees on the other side. One day, a small boy slipped while he was climbing the apple tree, and he fell onto a pile of sharp branches, cutting himself badly, and breaking his ankle. Alone and afraid, the young boy lay crying for hours amidst the tumble of sticks. Finally, the owner of the property happened by. He came out and lifted the boy from the branches. The child was afraid of the wrath of the farmer who had posted such ominous signs, but the old gentleman merely smiled at the boy and said, "I didn't put the signs up to be mean. I put them there to try to keep things like this from happening. It was kindness which caused me to want to protect little boys just like you."

Our loving heavenly Father gives us rules for the same reason. He is hoping to save us from pain and suffering. When we ignore His guidance, we find ourselves in terrible situations. We can feel confident that God is trying to protect us by His rules. He protects us from strangers who would prey on us and strangers who might mistreat us.

PRAYER: Dear Father, help me to accept the rules You have given me. Guide me that I might always avoid the snares of strangers, and the dangers in life. Amen.

DAY 18

Drink waters out of thine own cistern,
and running waters out of thine own well (5:15).

Two young men had been friends since early child-hood. They had shared everything. They had gone through the same experiences, and they understood each other perfectly. They were closer than many brothers. No better friends could be found. When they went off to college, they became roommates. Soon after college began, one of the young men fell in love with a beautiful young co-ed. The other man became jealous of his friend, and so he too began to woo the young woman, but behind his friend's back. When his friend finally caught on to what was happening, that friend-ship came to a bitter and hurtful end.

Fidelity, honesty, loyalty, kindness; all of these are attributes of God that we should desire in our own lives. When we violate these principles, we must pay a price. Greed and covetousness result, and they lead to ruin. It is best to always find contentment with "the waters of our own cisterns"—those things which are ours, given us by God. When we learn to be satisfied with what we have, then we avoid the pain and suf-fering attached to taking from others what is rightfully theirs.

PRAYER: I have been given so much that is good in my life, Almighty God. Make me appreciate what I have and stop longing for things which are not mine to have. Grant that my spirit might be satisfied this day, O Lord. Amen.

DAY 19

Let thy fountain be blessed: and rejoice with the wife of thy youth. Let her be as the loving hind and pleasant roe; let her breasts satisfy thee at all times (5:18–19).

While walking along the beach one evening, I saw an elderly couple strolling on the boardwalk. The man was blind, and his wife was lovingly leading him along. Her hands were gnarled with arthritis, and her legs were swollen. Both people looked as though they had lived difficult lives. Despite this, I could see the love with which the woman looked upon her mate. I walked up to the couple and told them that I was struck with how much in love they looked. The woman appeared a little embarrassed, but her husband spoke right up and said, "We've been married fifty-two years. I could never have made it without her. When everything else goes bad, I know I've still got the best little woman in the world to love me."

That old gentleman knew the real secret of happiness. It is never in the things we have or don't have. It's not in what happens to us or doesn't happen. The best thing in life is love. Those who are lucky enough to find someone to share their lives with enjoy a special gift from God. But for every person, the love of God is very real and very much freely given. We can be happy because we can know we are loved. Praise God.

PRAYER: O Lord, giver of life and giver of love. Though I am unworthy, I thank You for loving me so much. Help me to know Your love at all times, and grant that I might be able to always spread that love wherever I might go. Amen.

DAY 20

And why wilt thou, my son, be ravished with a strange woman, and embrace the bosom of a stranger? (5:20)

A young woman sobbed, "I just don't know what to believe anymore! I don't feel God with me like I used to." Her life had gone from bad to worse. She had followed in a long line of bad relationships and bad decisions. She had taken and lost a dozen jobs. She had moved from place to place and was swept up in every new fad to come along. She had joined a group of young people who gathered to meditate and chant together. It was the only place she felt accepted, but even there she found little comfort as her life crumbled around her. Throughout her childhood she had been a member of a church, and now she felt that she was every bit as devoted with her new group. Still, it wasn't enough.

There is no substitute for the truth and saving power of Jesus Christ. Other groups and sects may appear to be sincere and good, but they are "strange women" who lure us from what is right and good to things we should avoid. The Lord has said clearly, "I am the way, the truth, and the life: no man cometh unto the Father, but by me." (John 14:6) Other paths may seem good, but they are false paths which lead nowhere. Stay close to God, avoid "strangers," and all will be well.

PRAYER: There is so much that looks good to me, Father. Protect me from the things which would lead me far from You. Steer me back to You when I stray. Guide my steps by Your loving light, Almighty God. Amen.

DAY 21

*For the ways of man are before the eyes of the LORD,
and he pondereth all his goings (5:21).*

There was an eight-year-old boy who, like many other eight year olds, was terrified of the dark. One summer he went to stay with his grandparents. They lived far from the city, and so the nights were dark and quiet. The little boy would cower as the sun set, staying inside where it was light and safe. One night, the boy's grandfather asked him to come sit on the porch with him. As the boy hesitated, his grandfather moved over to him and laying his hand on his shoulder said, "I'll keep my hand on your shoulder the whole time. You don't have to go out alone." Under the watchful eye of his grandfather, the boy agreed. When they had stepped into the darkness, the boy asked quietly, "Why aren't you afraid, Grammpa?" The old man looked down and said, " 'Cause I know that God's hand is on my shoulder just like mine is on yours. Remember, boy, you never go anywhere that God is not right there with you."

It is good to know that we are never out of the Lord's sight. He watches all of our comings and goings. There is absolutely no place that we can go that God will not be, also. His hand is always on our shoulder, and He watches all our steps.

PRAYER: Be with me in every situation, Almighty God. Let me feel Your loving touch on my shoulder as I face the challenges of everyday life. Be my strength and my courage when I find myself lacking, Father. Amen.

DAY 22

His own iniquities shall take the wicked himself,
and he shall be holden with the cords of his sins (5:22).

A spider toiled along, crafting an amazing web which stretched forth eighteen inches squared. Once finished, the spider spun new webs connecting itself to the corners, until a labyrinth of gossamer filled the corner in which it stood. While the spider busily worked, a larger spider silently crept up alongside. At the right moment, the large spider entered the web, and the creator of it was trapped with no escape.

Sin is like a web. As we become occupied with the things we should not be doing, we become oblivious to the dangers that surround us. We feel that we are in control, when, in fact, we are in a very precarious position. We become "holden with its cords," and we cannot get loose. Ultimately, we must answer for our actions before God. If we do not repent of our misdeeds, they become a noose around our neck, and through our folly, we find ourselves hopelessly separated from God. It is good that we always pay attention to the ways we live our lives. It is when we grow complacent that we stand in the greatest danger of losing that which is most important. With God's help, we will never be ensnared.

PRAYER: Lord, I turn my attention to so many things which I should not. My sight is distracted by so much folly. Forgive me when I stray, and shine forth Your great light that I might follow its beam back to the source of all life. Amen.

DAY 23

For the commandment is a lamp; and the law is light; and reproofs of instruction are the way of life (6:23).

A man worked all his life at a mill which rested at the bottom of a steep mountain. Each evening, after a long, hard day at work, the man would begin his two-mile trek up the hill. Many parts of the road were steep and tiring. Sometimes the dirt would soften in the rains to a soft mud which sucked at the man's shoes and made the climbing all the harder. The man never complained though, for each night, as he neared the house, a warm friendly light shone forth from the window to welcome him home and guide his steps. From far away the light shined; first a pinpoint, but then growing larger into the full glow of a lamplight. For the man, there was no more welcoming sight in all the world. For him, that light was home.

As we grow in our Christian lives, the commandments and laws of God are like that lamplight to our eyes. They guide us and warm us and fill us with that little something extra which makes our travel easy. God shines His light brightly for all to see. It is within that light that we can truly be at home. There should be no greater feeling in our hearts than the warmth of God's love shining there.

PRAYER: Just as when I enter the light after being in darkness, it stings my eyes, so too I feel the sting when my sinful soul enters into the light of Your presence. It is a cleansing light, Father, and I ask that You clean my soul in the fire of Your most holy love. Amen.

DAY 24

*My son, keep my words, and lay up my commandments
with thee. Keep my commandments, and live; and my law
as the apple of thine eye. Bind them upon thy fingers,
write them upon the table of thine heart (7:1–3).*

There was a man who spent all his days sitting by an old
firehouse telling stories to the neighborhood children.
The youngsters would flock around the man to hear
him tell of bygone days. One striking feature of the old
gentleman was that around each of his fingers he had
tied a different colored string. The children would ask
what the strings were for, and the old man would say
that each one was to remind him of something important. This was the way he remembered things. But for
everyone who came to him, he had this to share:

"You don't need strings to remember the most
important things. God gave us ten fingers and ten
commandments, and if you keep one commandment
on each finger, then you'll never forget any of them."

The commandments of God should be as much a
part of us as the fingers which are part of our hands.
If we take care to remind ourselves of the laws of God,
then they will be forever inscribed on the very "table"
of our heart.

*PRAYER: I continue to forget the things I should do. Help
me to remember what You would have me do. I cannot
hope to be the person You want me to be without Your
help. Amen.*

DAY 25

I wisdom dwell with prudence,
and find out knowledge of witty inventions (8:12).

A powerful businessman was always looking for ways to cut corners. Any shortcuts and cost-cutting methods he could find, he would use. It didn't matter whether or not the cuts hurt quality or endangered employees. All that mattered was making the most money for the least cost. For awhile things worked well, but as time passed more and more people lost faith in the products that the man's companies produced, and finally he faced financial ruin. All the shortcuts he took seemed to lead to the reward he desired, but in fact, they destroyed the hope of reaching his dream.

There are no shortcuts to wisdom. The knowledge of the heart comes to us from patience, experience, and prayerful reflection. God wishes this wisdom for all of His children, but it comes only over time. Patience is a difficult virtue to obtain, but its rewards are greater than we can begin to comprehend. Shortcuts may look promising in the near future, but it is the person who learns the benefits of waiting who is on the road to true wisdom. It is so pleasing to God when He sees us grow spiritually, and the best way we can show that growth is to learn to say with Jesus, "Not my will be done, O Father, but Yours be done, now and forever. Amen."

PRAYER: Keep my feet on the right path, O Lord. Keep me from straying onto roads which seem to be easier to travel, but lead nowhere. As long as Your light shines forth before me, I know that all will be well. Amen.

DAY 26

Counsel is mine, and sound wisdom:
I am understanding; I have strength (8:14).

Solomon was considered to be the wisest of all human beings. His judgment was sound and fair. Subjects traveled from all over Israel to seek his counsel. His word was law because people believed there was no greater mind in all the world. Whatever Solomon decreed, the people gladly accepted. Solomon did nothing more than use the gifts God had given him in the best way possible. Solomon relied heavily on God's guidance and help. He prayed long and hard for God to inspire him with special wisdom. Solomon listened at length to the scribes who read the Scriptures to him. He was ever questing after a deeper knowledge of God.

Solomon was able to give great wisdom because he was in touch with the source of wisdom: God. As much as Solomon was willing to give himself to God, God was willing to give Himself right back. God showed that He was willing to do the same for us by giving Himself in the person of His Son, Jesus Christ. All we need do is accept His gift, and try to the best of our ability to follow His example. Like Solomon, we receive strength and understanding from the God who gives us all good things.

PRAYER: Lord, I wish I could be one with Your Spirit, that I might spread Your will in this world. You offer so much, and I take so little. Help me to use what You hold forth, that I might reflect the blessed light of Your Son, Jesus Christ, throughout this world. Amen.

DAY 27

*I lead in the way of righteousness. . .that I may cause
those that love me to inherit substance (8:20–21).*

A poor woman called her children to her soon before
her death. She sat them down and told them, "I
never had money or nice things, and I'm sorry that
I don't have good things to leave you, but I always
tried to do what was right by you. If I brought you up
right, so that you do what you know is right to do, then
I have left you more than any amount of money."

The woman was right. The things money buys are
temporal, they wear out, break down, and then they're
gone. A good sense of values is worth more than all
the money in the world. The greatest gift we can hope
to give another human being is that of wise counsel.
We often hope that we can leave a legacy—a testament
to our life—after we die. There is no more fitting legacy
than helping other people learn to love life and enjoy
it every day. We can make our lives an example of the
truth of Christ, letting others see just how much
Christ can change lives for the better. He will "lead us
in the paths of righteousness," but only so we might
have something of substance—something that will
last long after our material wealth has gone. That is
the real treasure, and God gives it freely to all who will
take it.

*PRAYER: I try to turn my eyes from material gain to true
gain: the gain of eternal life. Help me to follow Your
instructions, that I might have Your righteousness. Grant
me a small portion of Your holy inheritance. Amen.*

DAY 28

When he gave to the sea his decree, that the waters should not pass his commandment: when he appointed the foundations of the earth: then I was by him, as one brought up with him: and I was daily his delight, rejoicing always before him; rejoicing in the habitable part of his earth; and my delights were with the sons of men (8:29–31).

"Even if there is a God, how do I know I can trust Him?" a skeptical young woman asked. "I mean, we must assume an awful lot to think that He can know everything that is going on."

This poor woman suffers from a very common affliction: doubt. How can we know that God watches everything that goes on? We do so by faith.

Jesus Christ came that we might have a way to remove all doubt that God works all things for good. Christ assured us that God indeed watches over all people and that He reigns wisely and with justice. Christ Himself was present with God in creation. Christ dwelt with God, and when He came He proclaimed the truth of God for all people. The truth of God comes to each person individually through their relationship with Christ. If we will only open our hearts to Christ, we will no more need to doubt and question. We may rest in the knowledge that Christ is Lord, and that God is with us all the time.

PRAYER: O Lord of creation and love, You rise above time and space to dwell everywhere and everytime at once. You hear even my most quiet cry. Help me to trust in Your truth and reality. Answer my every doubt with "I am." Amen.

DAY 29

Give instruction to a wise man, and he will be yet wiser: teach a just man, and he will increase in learning (9:9).

A college professor laid out his philosophy of teaching on the very first day of classes. "If you will let me, I will teach you as much as I can in these few short weeks, but if you resist me, I guarantee that you will learn nothing. You won't like everything I tell you, but if you will follow my instructions, you will leave here much better thinkers than when you came in."

The professor was a taskmaster, who demanded perfection from his students. Many students, too lazy to put forth the proper effort, lost interest and complained about the strict grading and harsh comments. The few truly dedicated students found their professor to be one of the finest they ever had, and they valued his opinion above all others. This man helped them to be better than they thought possible.

God offers us the same kind of deal. If we will be open to His leadership, He will help us to realize our full potential. If we resist His help, then we can never hope to reach that goal. Wise men and women got to be that way by listening and trying to improve themselves. They are never content with who they are today, but they always look forward to what they can become.

PRAYER: May I grow a little bit today, and every day to come, Almighty God. Let me keep my ego in its place, never refusing to hear the things I should hear, in order that I might improve myself. Amen.

DAY 30

*A foolish woman is clamorous: she is simple,
and knoweth nothing. For she sitteth at the door of
her house, on a seat in the high places of the city, to call
passengers who go right on their ways: Whoso is simple,
let him turn in hither: and as for him that wanteth
understanding. . . Stolen waters are sweet (9:13–17).*

A flock of ducks flew south in perfect formation. They followed the powerful instincts to fly onward racing from the shifting weather, faithfully flying after the leader who showed them the way. Occasionally, the lead duck would spot a clearing with other ducks, and resisting the instinct to continue, he would lead his flock down for rest. In the safety of the clearing, they could find food, and energy could be restored.

At one point, a clearing appeared, and ducks bobbed freely in the marsh. The lead duck circled, leading the flock closer to the ground. Suddenly, the birds sensed that something wasn't right, but before they could climb higher into the sky, shots rang out, and many plunged into the cold water below.

When we allow ourselves to be distracted from our pursuit of God, the results can be disastrous. Sin, which leads us from our pursuit of the Lord, can pull us into situations that we don't want to be in, but before we can change them we are trapped.

PRAYER: Keep my sight on You, O Lord; clear my vision so that Your light is the only thing shining in my eyes. Protect me from the diversions and decoys which can lead me into ruin. Amen.

DAY 31

He that walketh uprightly walketh surely:
but he that perverteth his ways shall be known (10:9).

The stone face of the mountain seemed to stretch upward forever. It had a magnetic effect on the boys who had come to the camp. All of them were anxious to have the chance to climb to the top. The counselors warned them not to try it by themselves, but each year some foolish soul tried it anyway. This year was no different. While part of the group went to the ballfield for softball, two of the youths snuck off to attempt the climb. Before long they gave up, unable to master the tricky cliff.

The next afternoon, the counselors took the boys on the climb, and everyone made it. The older boys, who had made the climb hundreds of times before, guided the younger boys, telling them where to hold and where to step.

When we who walk this earthly road get into trouble, we often do not have the good sense to listen to those who have walked our road before us. There is nothing wrong with relying on the help of others to make it through life. God is the author of all life, and it makes sense that we should turn to Him in times of trial or difficulty. When we don't, we cannot be surprised that we don't make it through. Our help is always in the Lord.

PRAYER: I try my best to get through life, O Lord, but often I find myself at a halt. I don't know where to turn, where to step, what to hold onto. In those times, Father, help me to remember that You are there to guide me. Amen.

DAY 32

The blessing of the LORD, it maketh rich,
and he addeth no sorrow with it (10:22).

"As I grew up, I made a lot of mistakes," his grand-mother had told him before he went off to college. "I made foolish choices, and I hurt myself and others. There was one choice, though, which I have never regretted, and it's never paid me a moment of sorrow. That choice was to let the Lord Jesus into my heart. Don't you dare leave for school 'til you let Him into yours!"

Her words stayed with him, and it helped him a lot through the four years of school. He did make bad choices, and he did feel hurt sometimes, but he never felt alone, and he never regretted that Christ was in complete control of his life.

The love of God is something that no one should be without. It is the only thing we can ever receive that has no strings attached. It is given to us to give our life more meaning and brighten all of our days. There is nothing in our relationship to the Lord that can possibly cause regret or remorse. A good relation-ship with God is the path to true wealth, and it is a richness that nothing can destroy.

PRAYER: O Lord, You have made my life so wonderful. I am rich in a way that I never knew possible. I have escaped the worst possible poverty, and I praise You for giving me Your love so freely. Amen.

DAY 33

The righteous shall never be removed:
but the wicked shall not inhabit the earth (10:30).

The old apple tree had stood in the corner of the orchard for years. Its trunk was yards wide, and its branches stretched high into the sky. It had weathered many storms, even surviving being struck by lightning twice. It had long since retired from bearing fruit, but it cast shade over the yard and roof of the old farmhouse. Its roots dug deep into the soil, and nothing could move it from its place. The winds of time had long given up hopes of blowing it down, and the leaves thundered in defiance when a breeze kicked up.

As we dwell in Christ over the years, we lay roots which form a foundation which makes it impossible for us to be moved. Nothing can sway us if we plant ourselves completely in His love. If our roots are not in the Lord, we are shaken by the slightest thing, and we have no anchor to hold us in place. Christ invites us to take root there, we are there eternally, and nothing can affect us. We are nurtured and strengthened by the grace of God, and we can depend on growing strong and secure in His care.

PRAYER: I place the seed of my faith in Your soil, O Lord. Nurture and feed it so that it might take root and grow. Help my faith grow strong and tall in the light of Your love. Amen.

DAY 34

When pride cometh, then cometh shame:
but with the lowly is wisdom.
The integrity of the upright shall guide them:
but the perverseness of transgressors
shall destroy them (11:2–3).

Summer spelled freedom. The five young boys gloried in the unrestricted time they had. On one occasion, the boys found a pair of canoes by the bank of the river. One of them said, "Come on, let's take them out. Nobody'll know." Another boy said, "I can't go out. I'm not that good a swimmer." "Yeah, me neither," said another. "Aw, come on. You guys are chicken."

One of the boys gave in, but the other remained adamant in his protest. "You can call me any name you want to. I'm not a good swimmer, and I'm not taking the risk."

The other four boys pushed off and paddled far out onto the lake. As one of the canoes turned, it was struck by a series of waves, which tossed it over. Both boys were thrown from the boat. Only one resurfaced.

When pride causes us to ignore danger and do what we feel we should not, it can result in terrible trouble. Wise is the person who knows his or her limits and acts accordingly. God wants us to use the talents we have, and the first talent to use is common sense.

PRAYER: O Lord, watch over me as I try to do what is right. I act foolishly so often. Guard my steps. Grant that I might use the mind You gave me, in the best way possible. Amen.

DAY 35

He that is void of wisdom despiseth his neighbour:
but a man of understanding holdeth his peace (11:12).

As a child, I remember a man who lived down the street who frightened me terribly. He was an older man who was paralyzed on his left side. His face was disfigured, and he limped along on a cane. He had a low, gravelly voice, which he used to yell, "You brats stay away from me! Come too close and I'll split your head." For years I would race past his house, trying not to look at his face. I felt relieved when the old man died, but later in life, I found out how lonely and hurt the old man had been. He had lived a hard life, had no friends, and took his frustrations out in the only way he knew how. The man I had once thought was a monster was actually just a poor, lost soul.

I think often of how I misjudged the old man and feel foolish that I never tried to get to know him. I made judgments without knowing all the facts. It truly is the person who is without wisdom who despises his or her neighbor. Those who have understanding refrain from jumping to conclusions, and they hold their peace. There is so much good we can do, if we will only be patient and find out all the facts first.

PRAYER: I am too quick to judge, Almighty God. Grant me the patience and wisdom I need to live by the rule of gold; that I might treat others as I would like to be treated. Amen.

DAY 36

Where no counsel is, the people fall:
but in the multitude of counsellors there is safety (11:14).

All the young widow left behind was a note, saying, "I could have made it if I just had someone to talk to. I can't stand being all alone. I know my problems aren't so much greater than those of other people, but I need someone to help me solve them. I can't do it by myself anymore."

Out of desperation and loneliness, the woman took her life. This is the tragedy of those who don't know Jesus Christ. With Christ in our hearts we are never alone. God rejoices when we pour out our hearts to Him, confiding our deepest needs and desires. We all need someone to talk to. When there is someone to talk to, we feel happy and fulfilled. The load is taken off our hearts, and we are liberated. God is our Savior and protector. He listens to even the smallest of our cries. We can rejoice that we have someone who understands us so completely and cares for us so totally. When no one else is there for us to talk to, God remains by our side, never leaving, never turning.

PRAYER: My Lord, I need a haven in this stressful world. I need someone who will share my burdens and hear my cries. I need to feel that my cries are being heard. Hear, O Lord, the murmurs from the depths of my heart. Give me peace that passes understanding. Amen.

DAY 37

A gracious woman retaineth honour:
and strong men retain riches (11:16).

Judas Iscariot possessed qualities that Jesus considered worthy, or he never would have been selected as a disciple. Judas followed faithfully for the better part of three years, as he shared in the ministry of Christ. At a time when he should have been most strong, he proved weak. He gave in to the temptation of the sparkle of silver, and he betrayed his friend and Lord. He had lived so very close to the true treasure—the love of Jesus Christ, and he threw it all away due to his weakness.

Everyone sins. That is sad, but true. Often we are weak when we want to be strong. It is vital that we hold on to the love of God in those times when we are most sorely tempted. God offers us His strength when our own strength is not enough. All we need to do is pray for this strength, and it will be given to us. When we fall prey to sin, and we allow it to control us, we join with Judas in betraying the truth of Christ. When we call on God to help us in our weakness, then we have found true wisdom and strength. If we will deal honestly with God, He will shower us with treasure which cannot be taken from us, and honor which testifies to the glory of Christ.

PRAYER: O Lord, I pray that I might make You proud of me. I will try to please You by my actions and praise You with my words. Be with me, Father. Amen.

DAY 38

*They that are of a froward heart are abomination
to the LORD: but such as are upright
in their way are his delight (11:20).*

In a small midwestern town, a concerned group began
a crusade against pornographic materials being sold in
public places. Their protest met with resistance, so they
hired a firm to investigate the matter for them to see
whom they were really up against. By the time the
investigation was over, it came to light that not only
were area businessmen involved, but also the mayor of
the town, the chief of police, two school administrators,
and three powerful lawyers. The group gave up, as they
felt the deck was favorably stacked for the opposition.

Evil is a difficult thing to fight, and it seems
impossible to defeat when it is made manifest in a
large group of people. It is strange that evil forces
seem to have no trouble combining their strength,
while often the forces of good never manage to get
together. It is comforting to know that, in the end,
God's goodness is stronger than any amount of evil on
this earth. Those who are evil in the sight of the Lord
are an abomination, and they will have no part in His
heavenly kingdom. The upright are a delight to the
Lord, and it is those people who will dwell with God
in heaven eternally.

*PRAYER: Protect me from those who try to do me harm,
O Lord. In the face of evil, help me to remember that You
are God, and evil has no power over You, or those who
choose to follow You. Amen.*

DAY 39

There is that scattereth, and yet increaseth;
and there is that withholdeth more than is meet,
but it tendeth to poverty (11:24).

During the Great Depression, two families shared a
house in Pennsylvania. One family occupied the upper
floor, and the other family lived on the lower. The
family which lived downstairs was always inviting
people in to share what they had. When there was an
opportunity for them to help out, they would do so.
No matter how much they gave, they always seemed
to have enough. The family on the upper floor, however, scoffed at the way the downstairs family lived.
They stored all extras in a locker in the pantry. They
gave nothing away. It was not until they found that
rats had gotten into their pantry that they were sorrowful for what they had done. Interestingly, the rats
had not disturbed the downstairs pantry.

Selfishness leads to despair. True joy comes to us,
not from what we own, but from what we are able to
give to others. We were put on this earth to serve one
another, and when we fail to do so, there is a price to
pay. When we give what we have, God will bless us
with more, and the blessing will be double because of
the joy that giving brings.

PRAYER: Take what I have, Lord, and use it for Your
glory. I have nothing except what You have given me.
Help me to share from my abundance, and to give all that
I can to those who are in need. Amen.

DAY 40

A fool's wrath is presently known:
but a prudent man covereth shame (12:16).

The man impatiently looked at his watch. He was sure his friend had told him to be on the corner at 5:30 sharp. It was now ten until six, and he still had not shown up. The man grabbed his coat and briefcase and headed for home. All the way home he grew more and more angry. It was his birthday, and it had been tradition for him to meet his friend for an after work drink. They had done so for better than twenty years.

When he turned the corner and headed toward his driveway, he noticed the car of his friend parked in the driveway. Getting from the car, he slammed the door and stormed into the house. Seeing his friend, he flew into a rage. "Where were you? Some friend. You promised me that you'd pick me up. You lied to me!" The man's face was red with rage and hurt. So angered was he that he didn't notice the cake or the circle of friends who had waited to surprise him. An embarrassed hush settled over the entire group.

Anger can be a terrible thing. Everyone has the right to get angry, but it should never control us. We should be prudent and learn to hold our tongues, so that we might not embarrass ourselves and others by our uncontrolled wrath.

PRAYER: Help me to think before I react, Father, that I might not cause grief or pain. Let me learn patience and control so that my actions may be a glory to You rather than a shame. Amen.

DAY 41

There is that speaketh like the piercings of a sword:
but the tongue of the wise is health.
The lip of truth shall be established for ever:
but a lying tongue is but for a moment (12:18–19).

Words spoken in the heat of anger are spoken so quickly, but their impact goes so deep. Once said, words cannot be taken back. It seems to take many more words to heal than it does to hurt. It takes one unkind word to cut someone to the quick, but it may take a dozen apologies to make everything well again.

The words of our mouths are the reflections of our hearts. Like a fountain, we spring forth either good or foul water, depending on the source. If we keep Jesus Christ enthroned in our hearts, then we can rest assured that all of our words will be gracious, but if we continually take control of our lives back from Christ's loving hands, then we must take responsibility for words that may issue forth in anger or unkindness. Christ is willing to transform our hearts, to clean up the source of our life's fountain. When we give our lives to Christ, we allow Him to make us new. It is good to give our lives to Him daily, that we might always be reminded that He is the Lord and ruler of our hearts. With Christ in control, our words will be established forever, by the truth of Christ within.

PRAYER: Consecrate my life, this day, O Lord. Make me new, inside and out. Please be the ruler of my heart, dear Jesus. I am nothing without Your Spirit guiding from within. Shine through me, O Lord. Amen.

DAY 42

There is that maketh himself rich, yet hath nothing:
there is that maketh himself poor,
yet hath great riches (13:7).

He had worked long and hard and finally had enough saved for the stereo he'd always wanted. He had dreamed of this set for years. Now it was within his reach. The night before he was to go out and buy it, a knock came at his door. One of his closest friends came in crying and told him that her father had suffered a stroke, and that he was critical. She said she felt helpless because she was so far away, and she didn't have the money to get home. It would cost over four hundred dollars to make it. Hesitantly, he took the money from its resting place, and he gave his friend the amount she needed, plus a few extra dollars. He told her not to worry about it. All she had to do was go home and take care of her father. When she left, he found he couldn't be sad. The stereo would wait. It really wasn't that important. What was important was that he felt great inside.

Things lose value quickly when we make them more important than people. When we give what we have out of love for others, we come to know a joy beyond words. Selfishness kills the spirit, but giving sets the soul ablaze. We come in contact with Christ's Spirit the more we give to others and the less we think of self.

PRAYER: Take from me the things I have to give for others. All I have is Yours, heavenly God. Make me an agent of Your giving and love. Let me spread the joy of Your light to everyone I meet. Amen.

DAY 43

Poverty and shame shall be to him
that refuseth instruction (13:18).

A man who was very successful in business was asked what his secret was. He answered, "I never think I know everything. I'm always ready to listen to a new idea, and I always want to know when I'm doing something wrong." For forty years, he had been a top financial consultant, and he had a reputation for listening to even the youngest of colleagues. He never defended himself when he was rebuked by his superiors. He merely listened to the comment then did his best to improve.

This is the kind of spirit God wants in His children. God wants each one of us to grow to our full potential. Jesus tells us that we should be perfect as God Himself is perfect. The only way we can hope to move in that direction is to open ourselves to the constructive comments and criticisms of others. People can see from the outside things we might miss from the inside. Having the integrity and wisdom to seek out the counsel of others shows a definite desire to grow. We can do little else that is so pleasing to God. Only a fool refuses to listen to the observations of others. That person is too insecure to listen and too self-centered to want to grow.

PRAYER: *Dear heavenly Father, bless me that I might grow to my full potential. Inspire me by Your Word and by the example of Your Son. Fill me with Your Spirit so that I may more closely resemble You in all that I do. Amen.*

DAY 44

Much food is in the tillage of the poor: but there is that is destroyed for want of judgment (13:23).

The farmland was rich in minerals, and its produce was bountiful. The farm workers labored long and hard, and through their efforts, the yield was high. Unfortunately, the laborers received little recompense for their hard work. The farm was owned by a large corporation, and the residents were all hired by the farm at low wages. Their land was taken from them, and they in turn were made slaves to it. Most of the farm workers were on the verge of starvation, while they worked in plentiful fields each day. Their land was some of the most fertile in the world, but they were among the poorest of people.

Injustice should touch us at the very root of our soul. That part of us which is in God's image should be enraged by the unfairness in our world. And it should be the Christ in us which compels us to try to fight injustice wherever we see it. We may not be rich or powerful, but we do control our actions and our resources. We have the ability to refuse to support others who would take advantage of the poor. We can speak out against injustice, and we can offer comfort to anyone who is persecuted. When we do this, we have the joy of our heavenly Father.

PRAYER: Ours is a world of great injustice and inequality. Please guide me that I might work to change the way things are. Open my eyes to the plight of the poor, and lead me in the ways that I might combat it. Amen.

DAY 45

The heart knoweth his own bitterness; and
a stranger doth not intermeddle with his joy (14:10).

The woman was in shock at the death of her husband. They had been married for fifteen years, and she had settled into the idea that they would be together forever. She couldn't quite believe that it was true. Every once in awhile she would walk through the house just to make sure he wasn't there somewhere.

Her friends had been so kind and helpful, but she was glad they were gone now. She thought if she heard one more person tell her they knew exactly how she felt she would scream. They didn't know. They couldn't. Somehow it was different. She'd said the same thing on a number of occasions, but never again. It didn't do anything to help. Her pain was her own, and there was no way anyone could share it.

It is good to have friends that care, but we can have no friend greater than Jesus Christ. Christ dwells within our hearts, and so He is the only One who can honestly comfort us when our hearts are broken. Christ is as close to us as we are to ourselves. He is a part of us, and when we suffer, He suffers, but also when we rejoice, He rejoices with us. We are one with Christ, and it is so good to know that we never have to face life alone. He is with us in good times and bad, and He will never leave us.

PRAYER: Christ Jesus, You know me to the very depth of my being. Dwell within my heart, and grace it with Your strength and love. Let me feel Your presence within me. Guide me, protect me, stay with me, I pray. Amen.

DAY 46

Even in laughter the heart is sorrowful;
and the end of that mirth is heaviness (14:13).

She hated closing time at the bar. The crowds had thinned, and the lights were unplugged, and everything quieted down. It got too quiet. She had to face the thought of going back to her lonely apartment. She came to the bar to melt into the noise and laughter. She could be charming in the right setting. She could at least have a good time for a few hours, but it always came to an abrupt end and she had to face her desperate unhappiness. She sometimes wished she could find a party which never ended, but that was senseless. Eventually she would have to come back to reality, and her problems would all be waiting for her when she did.

So many of our attempts to find happiness end in futility. We look in all the wrong places for fulfillment and happiness. We exert such energy pursuing good things, and we never attain them. The deep loneliness that we sometimes feel inside is a homesickness for our Creator and heavenly home. When we take Christ into our hearts, we never have to face the loneliness which destroys. We stop looking for artificial answers, and we focus our attention on the one real answer: God. In Him, we find fulfillment and life.

PRAYER: O God, You have given my life such meaning.
I no longer seek other answers, for I have found the one
true answer. In Christ I have found everything I could
ever desire. Thank You, O Lord. Amen.

DAY 47

The poor is hated even of his own neighbour:
but the rich hath many friends (14:20).

I had a friend who got along wonderfully with me when we were alone, but when his other friends were with us, he treated me as if I were beneath him. He was wealthy, and so were many of his friends. They had their own language, and they judged people by what they owned, what they wore, and what they drove. One day, in frustration, I told my friend that either he could treat me the same way no matter whom we were with, or he could forget having me as a friend. To my surprise, he chose to end the friendship.

It is amazing how we find ways to judge one another. We set standards for acceptability and draw lines defining what is good enough and what isn't. We categorize people and force them into molds. This is wrong. We do our neighbor an injustice when we judge him. We are all children of God, and it is our purpose to see the face of Christ in all our brothers and sisters. When we treat another person as an inferior, it is as if we are doing it to Christ. Jesus taught us to love all people, regardless of their status. We are to accept everyone just as they are. When we learn to do that, we begin to love our neighbors as God loves us.

PRAYER: *Make me love everyone equally, O Lord. Help me to accept everyone just as they are. Help me to see my brothers and sisters as You see them, through eyes of unconditional love. Amen.*

DAY 48

A true witness delivereth souls:
but a deceitful witness speaketh lies (14:25).

There is a grand lady who stands in the New York harbor. Her name is Liberty. She holds aloft a torch which has been a guiding beacon to a land of freedom and democracy. Her witness is to a very special kind of truth. It is a truth that many people from many different lands never have the opportunity to know. It says that every person has the right to a full and happy life. True, it is an ideal, and there are many people in America who don't realize their rights, but it is a dream that is readily available to everyone who wants it.

God's people have ever been in search of a Promised Land. As Christians, we know that our Promised Land awaits us in heaven. It is the responsibility of every believer to bring about God's kingdom on this earth. We should walk in the truth of God. If we will devote our lives to His truth, then we can become the Christian nation that our founding fathers envisioned. The promise of truth in our land has attracted many, many people. However, when we turn from the truth, then the promise offered is just a lie. God blesses those who dwell in His truth. When we wrap ourselves in God's truth, we shine brightly, a beacon for the world to see.

PRAYER: Thank You for the dream of truth and righteousness. Let me be a part of that dream. Help me to shine forth the light of Your truth for others to see. Establish Your kingdom within our hearts that we might know Your truth here and now. Amen.

DAY 49

He that oppresseth the poor reproacheth his Maker (14:31).

A couple walked along a darkened street and came upon a young woman sitting with a baby in her arms. As they passed, the young woman held forth a hand and asked for some small gift to help her feed her baby. The couple recoiled from the girl's hand, and they hurried on their way. As they strolled along, they realized that they were not alone. Another person followed them. They quickened their pace, but the figure stayed right behind them. Finally, in frustration and fear, the man turned to the stranger and asked him what he wanted. The stranger replied, "You have had the chance to feed the Son of God, and you have turned away. Therefore, if you would hope to come into God's glory do not be surprised if He turns from you." With that the stranger walked away.

Christ said that when we help others who are in need, it is the same as doing it for Him. All of God's children were created in His image. When we reject any one of God's children, it is as if we are rejecting Him. He wants us to give from our abundance to make life more comfortable for one another. When we see the world through the eyes of God, we have compassion on the poor and suffering, and it becomes our heart's desire to help them.

PRAYER: You have put me here with a purpose, O Lord, and it is to learn to serve You. I can best serve You by meeting the needs of those I see in need around me. Grant that I may never turn away from someone in need. Amen.

DAY 50

Hell and destruction are before the LORD: how much more then the hearts of the children of men? (15:11)

A light plane crashed in the desert. The pilot survived the crash and began a long, hot trek toward civilization. He wandered for hours without seeing anything remotely man-made. As day turned to night, he began to think he had survived the crash just to die a slow, painful death. With morning light, he set out once more in search of rescue. When his last ounce of strength gave out, he sat down and began to cry. His sobs grew in intensity, and they merged with another sound. Controlling his emotions, he looked up to see a jeep approaching in the distance. He bowed his head to say a quick thank-you then waved to the driver of the vehicle.

There are times when we feel we must surely be out of God's sight, or at least out of His favor. It is comforting to know that God sees everything that goes on no matter where it is. God can see into the very depths of hell, so it is no great wonder that He can see into our hearts to know what we are feeling and thinking. Our lives are open to our Creator, and at the time when we think we have no hope, the grace of the Lord will reach down to us and let us know that we are saved. God will never leave us, no matter how far we may go.

PRAYER: Be with me, Father, as I walk along the many paths which make up my life. When I lose my way and turn from the one true path, wait patiently for me to return, and keep me ever in Your watchful eye. Amen.

DAY 51

A merry heart maketh a cheerful countenance (15:13).

"You never get mad. You always seem to be happy and having a good time. I don't understand it. I wish I could be like you." The two walked along the beach together. "It's really not that hard. You just have to decide that you're going to be happy, then do it. I got tired of being unhappy about everything, so I decided to quit," the other answered.

"It can't be that easy. There has to be more to it."

"It was that easy for me. I just thought about which I liked better: being happy or being sad. I don't like being sad, so I fight it."

We can decide to be happy. It takes work, but it is a conscious effort that anyone can make. God is the giver of the greatest joy a person can ever know. When we make Him the Lord of our life, He can work within us to fill us with this unspeakable joy. All we need to do is ask Him in. When we are filled with sorrow, we break the spirit, and we undercut the effectiveness of Christ in our lives. The Lord dwells in joy, and He is well at home in a heart that is happy. When we are truly filled with joy, the whole world can see it. They will notice that we are not like everyone else, and there is no more powerful testimony to the power of God than a smile which cannot be taken away.

PRAYER: Fill my heart with Your joy, O Lord. Change the light of my countenance to happiness so that everyone will know the effect You have had on my life. I praise You for Your gracious gift. Amen.

DAY 52

A wrathful man stirreth up strife:
but he that is slow to anger appeaseth strife (15:18).

The first pitch had been an accident. It had slipped from the pitcher's grip and had sailed at the head of the batter. Angry stares were exchanged, but nothing more. The very next inning, the opposing pitcher threw at the batter. The batter tossed aside his bat, and he charged the pitcher. Both benches emptied, and a brawl broke out. Players and coaches were ejected from the game, and tempers were allowed to cool before the umpires allowed play to resume.

It's a common occurrence, and a sad one. Grown men trying to start fights is silly, and it destroys the integrity of the sport. But once a person's pride is damaged, they will stop at nothing to get revenge. Spiteful people live to stir up strife. It is the prudent person, one who holds his or her anger, and stifles his or her pride, who brings forth peace. If we could learn to care less about ourselves and more about others, there would be fewer occasions when we would cause discord. It is the person who loves God who also loves peace. The peacemakers are the true disciples of Christ. To the person who refuses to stir up strife, there will come a great reward.

PRAYER: You have blessed the peacemakers, Almighty God. Please number me among them. Wherever I can be used, let me be an agent of Your love and peace. Send me where You would have me go, O Lord. Amen.

DAY 53

A man hath joy by the answer of his mouth:
and a word spoken in due season, how good is it! (15:23)

The algebra problem was a tough one. No one had given the right answer yet, and the teacher had gone through half the class. Andrea hoped the teacher wouldn't get to her. She wasn't sure her answer was even close. Smarter people than she had missed it. The most she could hope for was that someone else would get the answer before the teacher got to her. Her heart sunk, and she felt her cheeks flush as the teacher called her name. Timidly, she offered her answer. To her delight, the teacher praised her for getting the right answer. Andrea felt a surge of pride at her accomplishment.

It is a joy when we know we have done a job and that we have done it well. When we say or do the right thing, it makes us feel good. That is why God wants us to always do what is right. When we live a life of righteousness, then that good feeling never leaves us. We experience not only the joy of a job well done, but we provide a good example for other people to see. God is proud of us when we do what is right and good. We can feel great peace knowing that we are doing what God hopes we will do. His favor is worth more than all the riches of the earth.

PRAYER: I pray that my words may always be full of grace and pleasing to You. When I proclaim Your greatness and spread Your Word, I do what is pleasing in Your sight. Help me that I might forever do what You want me to. Amen.

DAY 54

*The wise in heart shall be called prudent:
and the sweetness of the lips increaseth learning (16:21).*

There was a small boy who always looked out for the feelings of others. Whenever the children would begin to tease or taunt another child, the small boy would defend the victim and offer comforting words. If a child fell or was hurt, the small boy ran to help. Whenever one of the children was in need of cheering up, the boy was right there with a kind word. All the adults said that he had the soul of an older man, and they claimed he was wise beyond his years.

Kindness is such a small thing, and yet too few people practice it. When a person is kind it causes others to sit up and take notice. The person who is kind and loving provides an example of what Christ wants for all of us. We enjoy being with kind people. They make us feel good, and they cheer us up. They are special people indeed, and it is well for us to join their ranks. God loves to see His children offer kindness to each other. Kindness is contagious, and we should always strive to cause an epidemic of loving and giving. Christians should be the first to be kind, to show the power of God in their lives to make a difference. Wisdom of the heart is the love of God, and it is the greatest gift we can hope to share with others.

PRAYER: I want to sow the seeds of Your love wherever I go, dear Father. Make me an agent of kindness and consideration. Help me to lift the spirits of other people and to make sure that they know joy all their lives. Amen.

DAY 55

An ungodly man diggeth up evil (16:27).

He knew he would find it if he looked long enough. His opponent could not be the saint he painted himself to be. Every man had a skeleton in his closet. They were unavoidable in politics. Once the public knew he had been treated for drug abuse in college, his pure reputation would be tarnished, and he would be brought back to earth. It didn't matter that it had happened thirty years in the past. All that mattered was that it had happened. It was all he needed to drag his opponent's name through the dirt.

It is sad that so many people take pleasure in the pain they can cause. God wants us to devote as much of ourselves as possible to loving other people, not destroying them. There is nothing good which comes from spreading rumors and trying to discredit those around us. When we live in the past, and in the sins gone by, we are chained to this existence, and we cannot move forward. Thankfully, God forgives us for the things we have done, and we can carry on with a clean slate. It is our duty to do the same for other people. If we hold the past against them, then we judge them unfairly. It is better to see each person for who they are now, and to realize that they, too, have been created in the image of God.

PRAYER: It takes so little to make others feel good, Father, and yet I don't try nearly enough. Make sure that I not only avoid doing harm, but also make me to do good whenever and wherever possible. Amen.

DAY 56

A gift is as a precious stone in the eyes of him that hath it:
withersoever it turneth, it prospereth (17:8).

The rain was coming down in sheets now, and she had
no idea how to change a flat. As long as it was raining
so hard she held out little hope of getting someone to
stop and help her. Suddenly, a rapping came at her
window, and she rolled it down slightly.

"Need some help?"

"I've got a flat, and I don't know how to fix it."

"You go wait with my wife in my car, and I'll have
it changed in a jiffy."

Her savior was a young man with a beard and a
kind face. He worked quickly in the pouring rain, and
when he was finished he was drenched to the bone.
She thanked him and began to pull a twenty dollar
bill out of her wallet, but he refused to take it.

"Listen, all I ask is that you remember this the
next time you see someone in need whom you could
help. Do something nice for someone else, and we'll
call it square," he said.

True kindness doesn't look for any rewards. It is
done from the heart, and there is no payment great
enough to cover it. It is only when we learn from it
and turn around and give it to someone else that kindness is repaid. Giving of ourselves to others is a precious gift, and when we give it, it just keeps on going.

PRAYER: Help me to give kindness, love, and care, Father.
Bless my efforts, that my gift may grow and spread. Amen.

DAY 57

He that covereth a transgression seeketh love; but he that repeateth a matter separateth very friends (17:9).

"You never let me forget, do you? Look, I said I was sorry a hundred times. I lied, I was wrong. It won't ever happen again!"

It happened every time they got into an argument. He knew he had done wrong, but he had asked forgiveness a dozen times. It would cool down, but then somehow it would come up and start another argument. If only he would let go of it, but no, he always held it over his head. It hurt to know that he wasn't forgiven. He had blown it and was truly sorry, but to be reminded of it over and over made him feel like a heel. He didn't know how much longer he could hear about it before it would begin to affect their friendship.

True forgiveness only occurs when we treat the subject as a closed matter. If we bring up old hurts whenever feelings fly, then we have never really forgiven. To hold a grudge is to build a wall between yourself and another person. Forgiveness breaks down walls. Christ came to break down walls and lead people to reconciliation. Before true healing can occur, though, we must let loose of all old hurts and start fresh. Forgiveness gives us the clean start we need to heal all wounds. With God's help, we can grow closer than ever before.

PRAYER: Teach me how to drop old hurts into the sea of forgetfulness and truly forgive those who have harmed me. Fill me with Your grace, that I might learn how to be graceful to others. Amen.

DAY 58

A friend loveth at all times,
and a brother is born for adversity (17:17).

He couldn't believe it. He had worked for the same company for almost thirty years, and suddenly they pulled the rug out from under him. It seemed like all his hard work had been for nothing. He had been a good employee, and he had never made trouble. Now he felt ashamed for no good reason. He didn't know what he would do.

A knock at the door brought him out of his deep thought, and he got up to answer it. Outside, his brother waited for him. When he saw his brother standing there, tears came into eyes. Whenever anything had ever gone wrong his older brother had been there to make him feel better. Just seeing him stand there made him feel like there was nothing to worry about. No matter what happened, he knew he could always count on his brother. He had yet to face any bad situation without his brother to support him, and as long as he could lean on him, he knew everything would be just fine.

As children of God, we can be thankful that we have Christ to call a brother. He will be with us in every situation. He will be our support and our counselor. He will listen without judging and will never leave us. He is as true as any brother could be, and we can count on Him to be there for us no matter what.

PRAYER: Thank You for being there when I need You. You are my strength and my shield. I am so grateful for Your love. Amen.

DAY 59

*Even a fool, when he holdeth his peace,
is counted wise (17:28).*

It took every ounce of courage he had to say anything. He had always been shy, and he was terribly afraid of being made fun of. He knew that if he ever opened his mouth, he would say the wrong thing and be ridiculed. He had been that way all his life. People probably thought he didn't know anything, and that wasn't far from the truth. He wasn't overly bright, and that just added to his fear. It came as quite a shock to him, then, when one of the girls in his class came to him for help with her assignments. She told him that she had always thought he was smart because he wasn't always talking and trying to impress everyone. What he feared most was that his silence would be taken as ignorance, while instead it was being perceived as maturity and intelligence.

We don't have to be brilliant, but it is important that we learn to keep our mouths shut when the situation warrants it. The wise person doesn't always have to be talking. They find comfort in silence rather than awkwardness. A fool speaks to cover silence and ends up saying silly and senseless things. The saying goes, "Silence is golden," and in many cases a truer word was never spoken.

PRAYER: I think that I have so much that is worth saying. Help me to remember that I learn more when I listen than when I speak. Help me to hold my peace, and to give others time to share their thoughts and feelings. Amen.

DAY 60

*Death and life are in the power of the tongue:
and they that love it shall eat the fruit thereof (18:21).*

Pilate looked out over the crowds of people. So, it had come to this. People who usually had no use for him were now coming to him, looking for him to pass judgment on one of their own. It was exhilarating to have such power. With a word, he could bestow life or death. The Nazarene seemed totally unimpressed by his power, but the crowd knew better. They knew that his word was law! No matter how many times he was called upon to pronounce sentence, he still grew tense with excitement. This was power, and he loved it.

There is power in our words. Our tongues are like two-edged swords. They can protect and defend, or they can cut down and destroy. We are in control of them. Sadly, many people act as if it were the other way around; that their tongues controlled their minds. As Christians, it is vital that we learn to control our tongues. James compares the tongue to a rudder. When a rudder is left untended, the ship flounders. Likewise, when our tongues move uncontrolled, the result is disaster. A wise person keeps a firm control over his or her words. Only words of life and light should be spoken, and with God's help we can hope to always have such graceful speech.

PRAYER: O Lord, take control of the rudder and steer this humble vessel. Use the words of my mouth to minister to the needs of others. Let the will of my heart always precede the words of my mouth. Amen.

DAY 61

Wealth maketh many friends;
but the poor is separated from his neighbour (19:4).

It was hard. All through college they had been the best of friends. They had gone everywhere together and done everything together. They had been inseparable. Since they had left college, though, things had changed. Her friend had married into money and taken a high paying job herself. Meanwhile, she was working with poor families, and her salary was barely enough to feed her and pay the rent. Her friend didn't seem to have any time for her anymore. They had so little in common. Really, the only thing that had changed was their financial status, but that was enough to drive a wedge between them. Her best friend acted like she wasn't good enough anymore.

Money can change many things. It can cause us to act strangely, and it can turn our priorities upside down. The interests of the wealthy are usually not the interests of the poor. The poor cannot hope to reach up to the level of the rich, but those with money have a great opportunity to reach out to the poor. God calls us to give what we can to ease the burden of those who are less fortunate. Money should never close us off from anyone else, but it should ever open new doors for us to enter into God's ministry.

PRAYER: Lord, all that I have has come from You, and to You I commit it. Let me use my wealth to build bridges, rather than to dig chasms. Help me to befriend others not on the basis of economics, but on their worth as children of Yours. Amen.

DAY 62

He that hath pity upon the poor lendeth unto the LORD; and that which he hath given will he pay him again (19:17).

A poor woman came to a rich young ruler and asked him for a few coins. The ruler turned her away, telling her to work for her food. A sick man came asking help, and he, too, was turned away. A friend who had come on hard times stopped and asked for assistance, but the young ruler told him to work for his wage. Then the Lord came to him, asking for a small loan. The rich young man said, "Lord, all that I have is yours. Take what you will, and more." The Lord took from the ruler and gave to the woman, and to the man, and to the friend. He said to the ruler, "I come to you in many forms. When you give to any of these, then you give also to me. Hold back nothing from those who ask, and your reward will be great in heaven."

It is hard to see sometimes, but when we give to a child of God, we give also to the Father. God loves to see us care for one another, and He abhors it when we turn away from others in need. The wise man or woman shares all they have and asks nothing in return. God showed us this way when He gave His Son to be our Savior, requiring nothing more than that we believe. This is the seed of true believing, and it is within reach of all who will take it.

PRAYER: I sometimes turn my back to the poor. Help me to remember that I am really turning my back on You. Forgive me for my unkindness. Let me learn to be unselfish, and take from me what is really Yours, Father. Amen.

DAY 63

The desire of a man is his kindness:
and a poor man is better than a liar (19:22).

Early in their marriage she had loved her husband's gentle spirit and giving nature. He had spent time with the children, and he had loved the free time he could devote to his family. As the years passed, things changed. He devoted more and more of himself to his job. He became obsessed with getting ahead. The pressures he felt at work he brought home with him. His once-gentle spirit had turned hard, and it appeared that he had forgotten how to give. She was very sad over the change and realized that part of it was her fault. She had grown accustomed to living well, and the only way their lifestyle could be maintained was through her husband's hard work. Deep inside, she wished that things would be different.

What we want inside will be apparent by the way we live our lives. Whatever we make our god, that we will pursue with all our heart, mind, and spirit. If the Lord is the desire of our hearts, kindness and love will show forth, but if we pursue material gain, or fame, or prestige, then we will be devoid of kindness and warmth. It is much better to forsake all wealth in order to live purely and righteously. God smiles upon us when we remain true to His ways. When we live for a life of kindness and caring, He rejoices.

PRAYER: Help me not to be swept up in the ways of the world. The path to heaven is a true path, and the reward is greater than anything this world has to offer. Amen.

DAY 64

*It is an honour for a man to cease from strife:
but every fool will be meddling (20:3).*

She wished she could be like her husband. Nothing ever seemed to get to him. He took everything in stride, and he acted as though he hadn't a care in the world. She, on the other hand, worried about everything. She was positive that if there was something that could possibly go wrong, it would. She didn't mean to be negative, but she couldn't help it. She wanted to be able to let go of her doubts and fears, but so far she hadn't been able to.

It's sometimes hard to realize that God gave us life as a gift. Many times it feels like such a burden. God never wants us to suffer unnecessarily. Part of the message that Christ brought to this world was that no one has to face problems alone. God is with us always. Another part of His message was that nothing on this earth is important other than our relationship to God and to our neighbor. Job, finances, illness, and a hundred other things create stress in our lives, but when compared with the bigger picture of eternal life, they are totally insignificant. As Christians, we need to learn to look at the world through eternity-eyes, rather than temporal-eyes. Our home is in heaven, and everything that happens to us now means nothing, as long as we have our relationships in order.

PRAYER: Lord, I get sidetracked so easily. I let the silliest things bring me down. Help me to see everything in its proper perspective. Grant me peace of mind which never ends. Amen.

DAY 65

Divers weights, and divers measures,
both of them are alike abomination to the LORD (20:10).

She stormed into the classroom with her paper clenched in her fist. She marched up to the professor's desk and tossed her paper in front of him. A "C+" was scrawled across the head of the paper.

"Why was I given this grade? This is a good paper."

"Good for anybody else maybe, but not for you. You put forth average effort, and you got an average grade."

"That's not fair. My paper is better than most in the class, but a lot of people got 'A's."

"Look, I can give you any grade I please. I think you can do better, so I gave you a 'C+'. That's it!"

"I'll fight it. It's not fair for you to judge some people one way, and other people differently."

It is frustrating to feel like we will be treated unfairly. By the same token, we should be very careful in our dealings with other people to be sure that we always deal with equality and fairness. Partiality is an abomination in the sight of God. We must always strive to do what we know is right.

PRAYER: Lord, let me look upon every person I meet as an equal. Help me to remember to treat them as I would like to have them treat me. Guard that I do nothing to offend or cause suffering. Amen.

DAY 66

The hearing ear, and the seeing eye,
the LORD hath made even both of them (20:12).

He stood looking on in awe. His son, his firstborn, was coming into the world, and he was a part of it. He had often doubted whether God existed, but now all of his doubts were gone. He looked on at the perfect little creation. Each finger and toe was a testament to God's loving existence. The miracle of life was overwhelming. It was inconceivable that something like this could happen by chance. Only a master artist of incomprehensible power and glory could come up with something so fine as human life.

When we look at God's creation, it is difficult to question anything about Him. There is so much to wonder at in the world. As we learn more and more, it should not make us skeptical of God. Quite the contrary, it should convince us that there is a grand author to all creation, and that His power is far beyond our wildest imagination. Only a foolish person would deny God's existence in the face of such remarkable evidence. To see God, all we must do is open our eyes and look around. His signature is on each one of His creations. He is right there for the person who has eyes to see, and ears to hear.

PRAYER: *O Lord, You are indeed everywhere. I look to the sky, and Your beauty and wonder meet my eye. I look around, and I see You in the faces of those I meet. I look inward, and thankfully, I see You in my heart. Amen.*

DAY 67

Bread of deceit is sweet to a man; but afterwards his
mouth shall be filled with gravel (20:17).

His boss had told him that he had to make contact with all twelve of the outlet stores. He struggled through ten then decided he'd had enough. He never did get back to the other two, but when his boss asked him, he said he'd completely finished. All went well until his boss asked him for detailed reports on all twelve of the outlets. He had no idea what he could say about the two outlets, and he didn't have time to get to them before the reports were due. He falsified the reports he turned in, but afterward he felt uneasy. He continually wondered if his boss knew what he had done, and it put unusual pressure on their relationship.

When we live a lie, it takes control of us, and it usually leads to more lies. We get caught in a tangled web, and we are continually afraid that we might be discovered. It takes so much more energy to tell a lie than it does to tell the truth. We may not like the consequences of telling the truth all the time, but it is much better than facing the consequences of being caught in a lie. Our God is the God of Truth, and those who live in lies will have no part in Him. The truth is a much better companion, and it will lead us straight to the gates of heaven.

PRAYER: I gain nothing through deception and lies.
Lead me in the paths of truth and righteousness. Help me
to see that a single grain of truth is preferable to a moun-
tain of lies. Teach me Your ways, O Lord. Amen.

DAY 68

Meddle not with him that flattereth with his lips (20:19).

A man was seen coming and going from a married woman's house. Her neighbor watched with fascination and concocted elaborate tales which she shared with her friends as truth. There was no evidence any more incriminating than the fact that the young man came regularly, but the rumor was that the woman was having an affair. The "news" spread like wildfire, and wind of it eventually got back to the woman's husband. He confronted her in anger and hurt. The woman defended herself well. The young man she was seeing was her own brother, who came to the house to study in between his classes. The senseless words of gossip caused unnecessary pain to other people and planted a seed of doubt which caused great trouble.

There is no such thing as harmless gossip. It is talking about someone in a negative way who has no chance to defend himself. It is usually based on half-truths and sparse information. It isn't done to build someone up. It is only done to tear someone down. When we tell false stories about another person, we are stealing from them in the worst way. We take away dignity and honor, and we throw dirt on their reputation. It is an evil that God despises because of its basic cruelty. Lovers of the Lord are lovers of all His children. Therefore, we should speak of our sisters and brothers only as we would speak of the Lord, Himself.

PRAYER: May my words be ever praiseworthy. Let no foulness or gossip pass from my lips, O Lord. Amen.

DAY 69

Every way of a man is right in his own eyes:
but the LORD pondereth the hearts (21:2).

Timidly, the man walked up to the pearly gates and cleared his throat. St. Peter peered at him from a high stool. Without a word, he pointed the man through a huge door and inside was a throne. The man walked to the throne and said, "I'm ready for heaven, sir."

"What makes you think so?" a voice asked.

"Well, sir, I gave to the poor, I went to church, I never cheated on my wife, I didn't drink, and I prayed twice a day."

"You mean, you got tax deductions, you wanted people to think highly of you, you were afraid you'd get caught, you were allergic to alcohol, and you said grace before meals, don't you?"

"I was hoping you wouldn't know the difference," said the man.

Not only are our actions important, but our reasons for them are important, too. God sees us not as we appear to be, but as we really are. He knows every motivation for every move we make. We can't kid God, and we shouldn't try to. We may think we are doing alright if we do the things God asks, but more importantly, we need to do what He asks for the right reasons.

PRAYER: Eternal God, search the depths of my heart to see if I am doing all I can for the right reasons. Lead me to new ways of serving You. Help me to see what is lacking in my life, and support me as I try to change. Amen.

73

DAY 70

A good name is rather to be chosen than great riches,
and loving favour rather than silver and gold (22:1).

Everyone loved Mr. B. He was a friendly old man who loved to play with children. Rumor had it that he was a brilliant man who could have done anything he wanted, but one day he walked out on his high paying job and he never returned. Instead, he stayed home, began playing with the neighborhood children, and that had been how he'd spent his days ever since. If a child was sick, he was right there to visit them. If a child was hurt, he was there first to offer aid. If the familiar ringing of the ice cream truck sounded in the distance, Mr. B. was the first in line, ready to treat the neighborhood children, no matter how many of them there were. His only purpose in life seemed to be to spread joy to the children he met. He never had a cross word, and he let them know that he loved each and every one of them. He was a legend.

When we give of ourselves, we find out what it really means to be rich. Life takes on new meaning, and we are filled with a feeling beyond description. God put us all here, and it is wonderful when we work together to make this life a joy. People who live to love others are a blessing to the Lord. In those people, we can understand what it truly means to be happy.

PRAYER: Teach me what it means to be happy, Father. You are the source of all that is good and right. Let me dwell within Your love, and let me be a channel for Your love in this world that needs it so very much. Amen.

DAY 71

Thorns and snares are in the way of the froward:
he that doth keep his soul shall be far from them (22:5).

The path looked like it would take forever. The house was just over the ridge, but the path wound all the way around the other side of the hill. The climb looked easy enough to go straight across. They left the path, and started up the incline. The growth was thick and the footing was treacherous. As they reached the top, the way was blocked by thorn bushes and stickers. They were too dense to push through, but when they turned to leave, the soft earth shifted, and they pitched into the brambles. The more they struggled, the worse the thorns stabbed and cut. By the time they made it back to the house, they were cut, bleeding, and exhausted.

Sometimes, the easy way is not so easy. When we look for shortcuts, we need to be aware of the dangers along the way. With our Christian pilgrimage, we can be sure that God knows the best way for us to go. If we will trust His guidance and help, then we can be sure that the path we are on is the right one. He will never lead us wrongly. The only time we get into trouble is when we go off on our own, exploring places to which God does not lead us. As long as we always know to return to His path, everything will be okay.

PRAYER: I am tempted to walk many roads, not just the one I am on. Many seem to lead to exciting places, and others look so much easier than the one I am on. Help me to know that You have brought me to the best place I could possibly be. Amen.

DAY 72

Rob not the poor, because he is poor:
neither oppress the afflicted in the gate:
for the LORD will plead their cause (22:22–23).

A man walked by a newsstand and looked over the magazines. He selected a couple of titles and prepared to pay for them. When he pulled out his wallet, he realized that the proprietor was blind. He looked at the stack of magazines and papers, and he selected a couple more. He then told the man that he had selected one, and that the price was $1.75. He paid the man with two one-dollar bills, grabbed the four magazines, and strode away whistling. He called back over his shoulder, "Keep the change," and continued on his way, happy at the deception he had just pulled off.

There are people who look for ways to take advantage of anyone and everyone they can. They take delight in kicking others when they are down. They are cunning, ruthless, and merciless. God will have nothing to do with anyone who lives by abusing the poor and helpless. God is on the side of the meek, and when they are attacked, God is attacked. The poor may not be able to defend themselves, but God certainly is. He will remember those who work to spoil the afflicted, and He in turn will spoil their souls. God is love, and those who live by hatred and evil will have no reward from Him.

PRAYER: You have blessed the meek and the poor and those who mourn. Let me be among Your blessed, Lord. I rejoice when Your will is done. Let me spread Your love wherever I roam. Amen.

DAY 73

Through wisdom is an house builded; and by understanding it is established: and by knowledge shall the chambers be filled with all precious and pleasant riches (24:3–4).

She loved visiting her friends. It was a joy to enter a place where there was so much love and affection. They spoke to one another with respect, and they showed kindness beyond belief. Even when the girls did something wrong, they were treated with love and care. She wished she could live in a home like that, and she swore that when she was a parent, she would try to be as fair and loving as her friends' parents were.

Families should be havens of love and support. We should learn what love is all about from our families. We should also learn what it means to truly love others, whether they deserve it all the time or not. Unconditional love means love which doesn't ask anything in return. Christians are called upon to love all people, regardless of whether they are worthy of it. This is the love which God gives to each one of us, and it is a love He hopes we will use in our relationships here on earth. A house which is built upon kindness and understanding is a fortress against all the evil in the world. A good home is a blessing beyond words. Establish a home in true love, and its benefits will last forever.

PRAYER: Teach me what it means to love unselfishly, dear God. Help me to judge no one, and to love everyone that I can. Forgive me when I am unloving, and fill me with Your Spirit, that I might grow in Your ways. Amen.

DAY 74

A wise man is strong;
yea, a man of knowledge increaseth strength.
For by wise counsel thou shalt make thy war:
and in multitude of counsellors there is safety (24:5–6).

The story of David and Goliath is a comforting one. Its moral says clearly that might does not always make right. If we will use our heads, we can overcome seemingly impossible odds. There was no question that Goliath was more powerful than David, but David proved to be the better warrior because he knew how to use his head, and he knew how to use his faith.

There are times in the lives of each of us when we feel like we don't stand a chance. We are overwhelmed by the immensity of our troubles, and they bury us under feelings of futility and despair. If we try to face these problems on our own, we will probably fail. The wise person seeks support in difficult times. There is no better place to turn than to the Lord. He will support and strengthen us in every situation. His counsel is solid and true. If we will join forces with God, then there is nothing on earth which can defeat us. Like David, we can rest assured that God will stand beside us. Through faith, we can be made victorious over even the most powerful forces on earth.

PRAYER: I am weak, Father, but I have no fear for I know that You are strong. I have nothing to fear in this life, as long as I listen for Your wise counsel and have the wisdom to heed Your loving advice. Be with me, I pray. Amen.

DAY 75

Fret not thyself because of evil men,
neither be thou envious at the wicked:
for there shall be no reward to the evil man (24:19–20).

It made him so mad sometimes. He worked diligently at his job, doing everything in his power to make sure that each thing was done right. However, the man he worked with could have cared less. If things were substandard, it didn't bother him at all. What made it really bad was that the rest of the company respected the work that the pair produced. No one knew that it was all because of him that things were done well. His partner was more than willing to share the glory, but he wouldn't carry his end of the load.

His efforts were not in vain, nor did they go unnoticed. When promotions came around, he was moved up into a managerial position, while his former partner stayed right where he was.

Often, it seems like the wrong people get all the glory. We try to do our very best, and we receive no credit at all. It is good to know that our Father in heaven knows everything that is going on, and one day we will be promoted to our heavenly reward. God blesses those of His children who do what they know they should. Those who slack off can hope for nothing more than His wrath, for He will not abide by the person who gives less than their very best.

PRAYER: I want to do the best in every situation. Help me to find my full potential and to use it in Your service. Lead me where I need most to go, and show me how I can be of the most usefulness. Amen.

DAY 76

*I went by the field of the slothful, and by the vineyard of
the man void of understanding; and, lo, it was all grown
over with thorns (24:30–31).*

Everyone remembered the property in its glory days.
The house was enormous, and it was beautiful. The
lawn had always been well groomed, and there was a
magnificent garden in the back. Now it was a dis-
grace. The lawn looked like a field, the house was
dirty, and the mortar was crumbling from between the
bricks. Vines covered the face of the building, and the
backyard looked like a garbage dump. The new owners were rarely home, and they did little to keep the
property up. In the three years they had lived there,
they had not mowed the yard once. The neighbors
complained, but the residents said they had the right
to live any way they chose.

Although it is wrong to judge a person based on
appearance, often we can get an indication of what
people are like on the inside by watching from the outside. If we live a holy life, it will be apparent in the way
others see us. If we are slothful, others will be able to
tell just by looking at us. Sometimes there are extenu-
ating circumstances which cause even the most upright
people to be negligent, but usually a person who is dis-
ciplined and committed to God will make every effort
to put forth a good example.

*PRAYER: Father, let what is in my heart be obvious to
all who might look. Let my outside reflect the goodness
which You have put inside. Amen.*

DAY 77

*As the bird by wandering, as the swallow by flying,
so the curse causeless shall not come (26:2).*

The memorandum said that the front office was displeased with the performance of some of the employees. One of the girls became really upset when she read the notice, but the girl next to her seemed unconcerned. She walked over to the girl and asked why she was untroubled by the message.

"The only people that the message is speaking to are the ones who are giving less than their best effort. I come here every day and give 100 percent. I know that I'm doing the best job I can. As long as I know I'm not goofing off, then I don't care what they have to say about it. If you're doing all you can, then relax. If not, take the memo as constructive criticism and do better."

When an insult or comment is directed to us, we need to weigh it carefully. If it is valid, we should act on it, but if it is unfair, then we need not be troubled by it. God asks that we try to be the best we can be. If we are true to our abilities, then He will be pleased with us. To the person who does all that they are able, an insult is like a bird that never lands, that never hits its target. While it is aloft it can do no harm.

PRAYER: When I do all that I can, make me secure in that knowledge. When I am doing less, help me to see ways to improve and grow. Help me to handle insults with grace, and let me not be troubled by comments which are not true. Amen.

DAY 78

Where no wood is, there the fire goeth out: so where there is no talebearer, the strife ceaseth (26:20–21).

The foreman was always finding fault with everything that was done. Nothing was ever good enough. Even when it was done exactly as he specified, it still wasn't correct. Everyone lived in fear that they would be his next victim. Some people dreaded coming into work for the fear of having to face him. That was why everyone breathed a sigh of relief when he went on a two-week vacation. From the first day the atmosphere changed in the office. People could breathe easily, and they got along much better. They stopped being defensive, and production increased greatly. When quality control came to find out why, they decided to replace the foreman, and the office became a joyful and peaceful place to work.

Some people live to stir up trouble. They cause so much pain and anxiety that they are despised. If we will be steadfast and endure the burden of such people, God above will see it, and He will reward us. There is no place with God for a person who intentionally inflicts pain on other people. A fire cannot burn without fuel, and so it goes that anxiety cannot continue without a cause. God will be faithful to remove the source of our pain if we will but rely on Him.

PRAYER: My Lord, I hope that I have caused no one pain this day. If I have, I ask Your forgiveness and ask You to lead me to a way that I can make amends to the person I wronged. Let my witness be one of peace. Amen.

DAY 79

Whoso diggeth a pit shall fall therein: and he that rolleth a stone, it will return upon him (26:27).

She couldn't believe what was happening. She had accepted a date for Friday night from a man she was seeing off and on. Then, out of the blue, her boss had asked her out. She had dreamed of that happening ever since she got the job. She reluctantly called her date for the evening and told him that she had become very ill, and that she wouldn't be able to go out. Then she prepared herself for her evening with her boss. It was a wonderful evening, and she kept trying to tell herself that what she had done was perfectly fine. They were riding the elevator up to her floor, and she was anticipating a nice ending to the evening in her apartment. When the elevator doors opened, her sometime boyfriend was sitting across from it. He had come to spend the evening with her, because he felt sorry for her. Suddenly, the guilt of what she had done swept over her, and she began to cry.

Each time we tell a lie, we set a trap. Someone might find out. Most lies have the potential of hurting someone. We do not have the right to do anyone harm. God watches each of us to see whether we will commit ourselves to living lives of truth or not. When we choose correctly, He rejoices and blesses us richly.

PRAYER: I want to be an honest person, showing my love and respect for other people by my honesty. Help me to destroy that part of me which is prone to lie and deceive. Give me a portion of Your truth by which I might live. Amen.

DAY 80

Boast not thyself of to morrow;
for thou knowest not what a day may bring forth (27:1).

He thought of all the times he had promised his little boy that they would do something together soon. Play ball, sail boats, go to the zoo; it really didn't matter. He was always too busy, and so he said they would do it soon. He always figured they had a world of tomorrows, and he had really believed that they would do all the things his son had wanted to. It didn't seem possible. One day his boy was running and laughing, and the next day he was dead. Why hadn't he spent more time with his child? Why did he always say "later," instead of "now"? The pain and guilt rested heavy on his heart, and he knew that he could never know the joy of sharing those times with his little son.

We live our lives as if we have all the time in the world. That is so foolish. The only thing we are sure of is that we have today, this minute. It is the wise man or woman who learns to live each day to the fullest. We must strive to be as good as we can be, and to give as much as we are able every single day, for we do not know which one might be our last. God richly blesses those people who will live fully and for the day. His pride is in His children who act wisely and don't waste any of the precious time He has given them.

PRAYER: Lord, help me to make the most of this day. Teach me to live a full life, and to do everything in my power to please You. Bless my life, Father, and make me a blessing in the lives of others. Amen.

DAY 81

As in water face answereth to face,
so the heart of man to man (27:19).

It was nice to get away from the city to spend a day at the lake. The sky was crystal clear, and the bright sunshine felt wonderful. The trees were in full color, as the cool days came on. They walked along the lake, which was smooth as glass. The view across the lake was mirrored perfectly on its surface. The reflection caused the beauty of the view to be doubled. The image on the lake was just slightly out of focus, and in places it rippled. The colors weren't quite as brilliant, but it was still exhilarating.

The image reflected back from water is slightly imperfect, and it is not as clear as the object it reflects. The same can be said of one's soul. It is merely a reflection of the soul of God in which it was created. As we grow closer to God, the image comes into sharper focus, and it more closely resembles the soul of our Creator. The goal of Christians should be to become as much like God as is possible. All we have to do is let God finish the work He has begun in us. If we turn our lives over to God, then He will make us over in His image, and He will fill in the details which are lacking. He wants nothing more than for our souls to merge with His, so that both object and reflection are one.

PRAYER: Lord, I want to be one with You in soul, mind, and being. Help me to be the creation You want. Work through me that others may know Your great love and power. Amen.

DAY 82

*A poor man that oppresseth the poor is like
a sweeping rain which leaveth no food (28:3).*

The crops were almost in ruins. If rains didn't come soon, the people in the village would face another year of starvation. The forecasts had been dismal for so long that the people could hardly believe it when rain was predicted. The clouds began to form, the wind to blow, and the blessed moisture began to drop. But the storms kept building, and the winds increased. The water pounded the ground, and it beat upon the crops. The food supply which had so desperately needed water was completely wiped out by storms and flooding when the rains finally came.

We see the rich of this world oppressing the poor, and it seems almost natural, but when the poor do things to hurt each other it is amazing. It is as if they forget their poverty themselves and inflict worse on their neighbors. It is senseless and cruel, and it strikes with the force of a terrible storm. It is hard to defend or deal with, because it is so unexpected. We feel that the people most like us will relate to our plight and be sympathetic. Evil strikes in every place, though, and it is by God's grace that those who are faithful will at last be saved.

PRAYER: I do things which are cruel to the people I should be most kind to. Forgive me when I do such foolish and hateful things. Father, help me to be thankful for Your grace and love. Let my thanks be shown through my love for others. Amen.

DAY 83

He that turneth away his ear from hearing the law,
even his prayer shall be abomination (28:9).

He was always late to every meeting. His superiors
tried to get him to play by the rules, but he resisted.
His work was usually good, so they let him go. Lately,
though, they had entrusted him with some vital work,
and he showed no sign of trying to get it in on time.
He worked at his own pace, he skipped the progress
meetings, and he refused to talk about it to anyone.
When he finally produced the package to his firm, it
was a week late, and they were no longer interested.
He was let go without so much as an explanation.

When we turn away from the instruction of our
superiors, then we must be willing to suffer their
wrath. We are answerable to God in this life, and if we
choose to ignore Him, we cannot be surprised when
He chooses to ignore us. We cannot live any old way
we want to and use God only when we want something from Him. Our lives must be devoted to Him,
and we are called to walk in all His ways. We must
heed His instruction and guidance, and when we do
that He will be faithful to hear and answer our
prayers. He is so happy when His children listen for
His voice, and He will listen to us when we call out
to Him.

PRAYER: I am a proud person, Lord. I think that I know
what is best, and I sometimes ignore the suggestions of
others. Teach me to listen, to trust, and to obey. Hear this
prayer, this day, O Lord. Amen.

DAY 84

He that giveth unto the poor shall not lack: but he that hideth his eyes shall have many a curse (28:27).

There was a poor family who decided it was beyond their means to celebrate Christmas. They told their children not to expect presents, they planned a simple meal for Christmas Day, they decided not to decorate, and they told the children the less said about Christmas the better. Some friends heard of the situation, and they pooled resources to give the family a Christmas they would never forget. On a day when the family went out, all the neighbors pitched in and decorated the house, putting up a tree, and surrounding it with presents. The refrigerator was stocked with wonderful treats and a feast fit for royalty. No indication was left of where the things had come from. When the family returned home they understood what Christmas was all about, and they truly did have a Christmas that none of them would ever forget.

It is important that we look for ways to give to those people who are in need. When we give unselfishly and totally, we begin to understand what God wants of us. God gave us the life of His Child, Jesus, and it is when we give of ourselves to others that we please God the most. We can never pay God back for His great gift, but we should try whenever possible.

PRAYER: Show me ways that I can do good things for other people who are not as fortunate as I am. If nothing else, I can pray for them and give them my care and love. Help me to give what I can whenever I can. Amen.

DAY 85

When the righteous are in authority, the people rejoice: but when the wicked beareth rule, the people mourn (29:2).

In a small New England town, a bank and a library prepared for the holidays. The week before Christmas, the library announced that there would be a party to celebrate a good year, and a Merry Christmas. The bank made no such announcement. The president felt that a Christmas party was beneath the dignity of a bank. He said that business would be carried on as usual, and that was that. The people in the library felt that Christmas had come early. They were appreciative of the consideration, and the atmosphere was happy and festive. At the bank, the people felt a sadness. The Christmas spirit had been stifled, and the atmosphere was heavy and gray.

It takes very little to make people happy. A little giving goes a long way. When we deny people even the smallest kindness, they lose spirit, and there is no joy. People rejoice under kind leadership, but harsh and unthinking leadership gives rise only to mourning. God loves a cheerful giver, and He doubly loves givers of joy. If we will remember the great love that God has shown us, it will be easy to show a little of that love to the people we deal with day in and day out.

PRAYER: Let me sow seeds of kindness, Lord, that people might know of my great love for You. You have given so much, now help me to give a little. Being kind is not hard, and it costs so little. Help me to give it freely and abundantly. Amen.

DAY 86

The bloodthirsty hate the upright:
but the just seek his soul (29:10).

The headlines screamed of the atrocity. A young woman had been killed while she was home for the holidays. She had been assaulted and beaten and then killed. It was shocking any time it happened, but there was something which made it worse at holidays. The woman's family would remember this every year when the season rolled around, and it would place a cloud over the celebrations.

The killer was caught just before Christmas, and the parents of the girl wanted to see him. They went into a room where a guard brought in the accused. For a moment they sat looking at each other, then the father said, "I don't know why you killed our baby, and I don't really care. I want to hate you, but I can't. God gave His Son so that I might have life, and now I've given my daughter. I hope that her life makes a difference. We came to tell you that we're praying for you, and we hope you really repent of what you have done. We won't stop praying until you're dead or saved." With that, the couple left.

How can we learn to love those who try to hurt us? Christ did it through the grace of God. God will supply us with the same power if only we will seek Him out.

PRAYER: Your gift to me in the life of Your Son is greater than I can comprehend. I want to know that love in my life. Help me to pray for the evil people in this world, that they might know the truth and love that You freely give. Amen.

DAY 87

The poor and the deceitful man meet together:
the LORD lighteneth both their eyes (29:13).

He hated having to walk to work. His office was in the center of a poor part of town. The beggars sat along both sides of the street, and he couldn't stand to smell their smell, to see their faces, or hear their pitiful begging. He hurried through the streets, and the question ran through his mind why God made him suffer like this? He wished the poor would go off and find some other street to haunt.

As he approached his office, he saw, from the corner of his eye, yet another group of poor people clustered outside a church. He walked past them, feeling outraged that they even littered the lawn of the church. He decided enough was enough. He turned to speak his piece to the group, but what he saw made him stop. His heart sank and he felt a pang of guilt and shame in his stomach. The group on the lawn was the nativity scene. The poor were Mary, Joseph, and the Babe, and suddenly the evil of his thoughts was made clear to him.

God has made us all, and He has made us equal. If we reject poor people because they make us feel guilty or uncomfortable, then we must remember that we would reject Christ Himself, who never made a claim to prominence or wealth.

PRAYER: Let me accept all people just as they are. Open my eyes so that I can see the Christ which exists in all of Your children. I love You, Lord; I want that love to grow as large and strong as is possible. Amen.

DAY 88

Seest thou a man that is hasty in his words?
there is more hope of a fool than of him (29:20).

The rush was on. The woman stood bewildered in the department store. Her husband had asked especially for a certain razor, and she was determined that she would get it for him. She finally got a sales clerk to wait on her, and she told him what she wanted. He looked at the counter and then went into a fast sales pitch for a razor that was on sale. Five times she repeated what she wanted, and five times he tried to sell her something else. In frustration, she walked away to try another store.

Sometimes it feels like no one listens to us. We try to communicate what we mean, but it never gets through. It is frustrating when we deal with people who will not listen to what we say, and they themselves never quiet down. When we listen, we learn. When we talk, we block learning. A fool loves to hear the sound of his own voice, but the wise person rejoices in what can be heard. We need to learn to listen, so that we can honestly help the people who come to us for our aid. If we talk, we will close people out and they will never come back. We deal foolishly, and we present an example that we cannot be proud of. God wants us to deal with people in love. People need to feel like they are being heard.

PRAYER: I know You listen to me, Lord. Teach me to listen that I might be a blessing to those whom I serve. It is in silence that understanding comes. Amen.

DAY 89

*There is a generation that curseth their father,
and doth not bless their mother. There is a generation
that are pure in their own eyes, and yet is not washed
from their filthiness. There is a generation, O how lofty
are their eyes! and their eyelids are lifted up (30:11–13).*

His parents were such an embarrassment to him.
They were old-world Italians, and they just didn't fit
in with his image. He had worked all his life to beat
the stereotypes, and he'd done his best to deny his
heritage. He lived in fear that his parents would show
up at the wrong time and spoil everything. He was
rich and popular, and he was ashamed of being asso-
ciated with his garlic-eating parents.

There is nothing more sad than a person who
rejects who he is and where he comes from. When we
get so proud that we deny our families, then we have
very little character or compassion. We should be proud
of where we come from. Whether we are Italian,
American, Russian, Black, White, Christian, Jew, or any
of a thousand other categories, we come from a single
source, and that is God in heaven. We should be proud
of that heritage. If we are proud of our heavenly Father,
He will be proud of us, and we will know a happiness
that will never, ever end. We are made holy through the
love of God.

*PRAYER: I am proud of You, Lord. How could I be other-
wise? Without You nothing which now is could ever be. You
have created everything, and You have made me special and
unique. I am Your child, and I will love You forever. Amen.*

DAY 90

She girdeth her loins with strength, and strengtheneth her arms.
She perceiveth that her merchandise is good (31:17–18).

She was an organizer. Everything had to be done in a particular order at a particular time. She knew she was a perfectionist, but it had always paid off. She usually got what she set her sights on, and everyone knew that she was dependable and trustworthy. If there was a job that they needed done by a specific time, they came to her. She was proud of her accomplishments, and it gave her a deep satisfaction to know that other people looked at her work to improve their own. She was an example, and she vowed that as long as she lived, she would be a good one.

In this day and age, not too many people are concerned with quality and integrity. Many try to get by with exerting the least amount of effort possible, and they refuse to give more than what is asked for. It is the wise person who knows to give all they can. God is hoping that we will be bright and shining examples of truth and goodness. When we give less than 100 percent, we provide a shoddy example, and we are an embarrassment to God. When we live our lives to the fullest, then we do God honor, and His glory is spread through our lives. God will bless us richly, if we will only strive to be the creations He intended us to be.

PRAYER: Lord, I sometimes let down and don't do all I should to make You proud of me. Help me to see ways that I can improve myself, and in so doing, bring honor and glory to You each day. Amen.

If you enjoyed this
Wisdom from the Proverbs
Value Book,
be sure to pick up the 366-day devotional.